A Closer Walk with God

David R. Mains

David C. Cook Publishing Co.

ELGIN, ILLINOIS—WESTON, ONTARIO

A CLOSER WALK WITH GOD
© 1980 David R. Mains

All Scripture quotations are from the Revised Standard Version unless otherwise noted.

Published by David C. Cook Publishing Co., Elgin, IL 60120
Cover design by Joe Ragont
Printed in the United States of America.
ISBN 0-89191-264-9
LC 80-51282

CONTENTS

1 Doing a Great Work
2 The Spirit of a Conqueror
3 The Possibility of Something Better
4 Be Careful, Little Eyes, What You See
5 Searching for a Mentor
6 The Wonder Drug
7 Good Soldiers and Deserters
8 Revealed by Fire
9 The Long Shadow of the Righteous

The Chapel Talks Series by David Mains

Making Church More Enjoyable
How to Support Your Pastor
How to Resist Temptation
God, Help Us with the Kids
What's Wrong with Lukewarm?
Praying More Effectively
Getting to Know the Holy Spirit
When God Gets Angry with a Nation
A Closer Walk with God
Psalms That Touch Us Where We Live
Making Scripture Yours
I Needed That Encouragement

Introduction

Most people listen to the radio while they're doing something else. As a broadcaster I'm aware that a person hearing me is probably shaving, fixing breakfast, driving to work, or some similar activity. Being able to keep his or her attention in such a setting is a lot different than preaching to a captive audience.

Therefore, I was dubious as to whether the slow pace of radio with its need for frequent repetition and underscoring each key truth would transfer all that well into print.

To complicate matters further, every time a program is made I must assume many listeners didn't hear what was said the day before. But just the opposite is true when compiling the chapters of a book. They build on one another.

Well, the first series of Chapel talks is now completed. Through the help of others, my broadcast scripts have been made more readable than I thought possible. The greatest thanks for this project goes to my wife, Karen, who put aside her own writing to help me out. Two Chapel of the Air staff members, Ruby Christian and Sharon Morse, also did yeoman duty typing long hours after work and on weekends.

1

DOING A GREAT WORK

If you visited me in my study you'd undoubtedly notice an old lithograph hanging on the wall. It's an unused advertising poster that normally would have died a natural death pasted to a barn or a fence. Three-and-a-half feet long and just a little over twelve inches wide, it reads, "Thurston the magician performs the world's most famous illusion—the East Indian Rope Trick." The major portion of space is occupied with a picture of smoke and a rope emerging from a large wicker basket. A turbaned lad hangs at its zenith, feet and arms entwined, enabled to stay in this amazing position by the powers of the commanding figure of a magician who stands nearby with his arms extended.

One reason I bought the poster some years ago in a used bookstore was because magic had been an active hobby of mine all the years I was growing up. But more than that, I had read quite a bit about various performers, including this man Thurston, whom many consider to be the greatest magician who ever lived.

As a poor newsboy in Chicago he dreamed of fame and wealth, but it must have seemed a long way off when he ran away from home to escape a cruel father. Trying his hand at being a jockey, a bellhop, and a gambler, at seventeen he found himself stranded and penniless in New York. Wandering into a gospel mission, he was touched by the message and responded when an invitation was given to receive Christ as Saviour. Two weeks later he was preaching on a street corner in Chinatown, happy for the first time in his life.

The youth felt God had called him to be an evangelist so he enrolled in D. L. Moody's school at Northfield, Massachusetts, working as a janitor to pay his way. At the same time, he attended evening classes to learn the three Rs since he had received so little formal schooling. In time, Thurston, who was very bright, decided the Lord was calling him to become a medical missionary. But something happened on his way from Northfield to begin his studies at the University of Pennsylvania.

Having a little time in Albany between trains, he strolled around the city. Strange feelings stirred within him as he passed a theatre where Herrmann the Great, a popular German-American magician and one of his boyhood idols, was performing. Howard bought a ticket, went in, and was completely captured by what he saw.

To shorten the story, Thurston never reached medical school. Instead he followed Herrmann to Syracuse and began learning sleight of hand. Eventually he

became successful enough to stage his own perfor-
mances and was almost immediately well received. A
little over three decades later, he had amassed a fortune
of two million dollars, traveled the world, and appeared
before royalty in many countries. With his repertoire
expanding every year, he performed at the White
House in 1924, arriving with twenty-two assistants, a full
orchestra, and truckloads of equipment.

A popular new volume of magic posters currently
offered by several large American Book Clubs describes
some of his acts as follows:

> As the beautiful girl slept in hypnosis, her rigid body
> suspended between two assistants, the great magician,
> covering the body with only a sheet, commanded her to
> float. The audience, in silent awe, gazed upon a seeming
> miracle as the figure rose and drifted across the stage, and
> over the footlights and the orchestra pit and back to the
> stage. The compelling voice of the magician continued its
> instructions and she turned in a complete circle, raised her
> right hand under the sheet and rose still higher. Then the
> magician stepped forward, pulled the sheet from the
> floating figure and she was gone!

Howard Thurston's reputation as one of the greatest
and best-remembered magicians rested primarily on
such illusions as the Floating Lady or the Phantom
Piano, in which an entire upright and its pianist disap-
peared on an empty stage with the music playing until
the last moment.

His version of the fabled rope trick shown on my
poster was one of his most costly illusions. Reportedly
he spent more than $10,000 developing it. Introduced in

the 1927-28 season, it was kept in the show strictly for its publicity value. Complicated to perform properly, it was not as effective as many other of his features even when it worked smoothly.

Thurston died in 1936, and now, years later, not too many people remember his name. More sober in the values of eternity is the thought that in some unenlightened part of an unnamed continent, certain natives waited in vain for a medical missionary to minister to their bodies and souls. Because he was diverted in his call from God, Howard Thurston never arrived. The wallhanging in my study has served as a reminder of the need to keep focusing on the eternal.

It strikes me that stories of being diverted from God's desires are common among the Lord's people. At some time during one's Christian experience, quite possibly not long after conversion, there is a strong sense that he says, "I have an important job for you." This could relate to a vocation in Christian service or a certain kind of involvement in the life of the church or community. Beyond just personal thoughts, the Lord bent close and said, "I need your skills for my work of ministry among the poor, or in teaching the handicapped, or dealing with the sick, or sharing your faith with others, or touching this situation or that one with goodness."

Now in reviewing what's happened since that time, it becomes quite clear that somewhere along the line you were diverted from fulfilling your divine personal assignment. Maybe other interests crowded in on your time, or your walk with the Lord wasn't strong enough to sustain your direction, or someone opposed or criticized your work, so you quit; or any of a thousand things happened; but the ultimate result was that you put aside that unique spiritual compunction.

God has many means of drawing people back to his assignments for them. Maybe he's using my words at this moment to cause you to reshuffle your priorities and see that his desires are not overlooked. Of course, I'm aware that factors like age or health often make it impossible for people to return to what once was. But I also know God is gracious, and if you draw close to him he will draw close to you and before long a new privilege of service will be impressed on your heart. What's important is that you not allow yourself to be diverted a second time.

A special section of Scripture I think can be meaningful right now is found in the Old Testament book named after Nehemiah, a Jew in exile and the respected cupbearer for the powerful Persian king Artaxerxes.

Hearing a report that the walls of distant Jerusalem were broken down, the gates destroyed by fire, and the remaining people in trouble and shame, Nehemiah became deeply burdened. There's no record of a vision from God; he just felt a strong sense of sorrow that led to fasting and to the eventual request to his king: "If your servant has found favor in your sight, that you send me to Judah, to the city of my fathers' sepulchres, that I may rebuild it" (Neh. 2:5). Scripture continues:

> So I came to Jerusalem and was there three days. Then I arose in the night, I and a few men with me; and I told no one what my God had put into my heart to do for Jerusalem. There was no beast with me but the beast on which I rode. I went out by night by the

Valley Gate to the Jackal's Well and to the Dung Gate, and I inspected the walls of Jerusalem which were broken down and its gates which had been destroyed by fire. Then I went on to the Fountain Gate and to the King's Pool; but there was no place for the beast that was under me to pass. Then I went up in the night by the valley and inspected the wall; and I turned back and entered by the Valley Gate, and so returned. And the officials did not know where I had gone or what I was doing; and I had not yet told the Jews, the priests, the nobles, the officials and the rest that were to do the work (Neh. 2:11-19).

In chapter 6, Sanballat and Tobiah, pesky antagonists through the entire narrative, sent a letter to Nehemiah saying, "Come and let us meet together in one of the villages in the plain of Ono" (v. 2). Four times such word is received. However, said Nehemiah, "They intended to do me harm. And I sent messengers to them, saying, 'I am doing a great work and I cannot come down'" (vv. 2, 3).

I like that verse. "I know what the Lord expects me to do and I refused to be diverted or intimidated by you. . . ."

Maybe it would be appropriate for you to adopt Nehemiah's attitude and words if God's Spirit has been speaking to you. This way they can become for you the same kind of a constant reminder the Howard Thurston lithograph in my study is for me.

You can't possibly miss what I've been saying. The thrust of my remarks can be summed up as follows: *Doing a great work for God requires overcoming distractions!*

2

THE SPIRIT OF A CONQUEROR

"The Spirit of a Conqueror"—that sounds a little like a comic book expression or something describing a hero in an epic film on television. Certainly, it's not a term we hear in everyday conversation. My contention is that the lack is to our detriment.

Now that phrase, fit into my key sentence for this chapter, comes out this way: *Mature believers manifest the spirit of a conqueror.* But before I continue I should illustrate what I mean by "the spirit of a conqueror."

Let's begin by comparing the apostles as they appear in the Gospels in contrast to the picture they present in the Book of Acts. For example, in the Gospels the twelve are sincerely interested in the Kingdom. They carefully observe Christ's life and teachings and cautiously decide to follow him. But in Acts, they've progressed far beyond sincere interest. These are now totally committed men.

In the Gospels, the twelve are fragmented and self-centered. Even near the end, James and John infuriate their companions by selfishly requesting places of honor at Christ's right and left hand when he comes into power. In comparison, less than halfway through Acts (chap. 12) James had given his life for the cause and there's a distinct sense of oneness among the remaining apostles as they become a spiritual entity.

In the Gospels, these men might be classified as novitiates. They ask questions such as: "Jesus, how can we possibly feed all these people?" As Acts unfolds, they're experienced workers. "Look at us. . . . I have no silver and gold, but I give you what I have. In the name of Jesus Christ of Nazareth, walk" (Acts 3:4-6).

The twelve are somewhat confused in the Gospels. Christ's parables need explaining. They see the Kingdom basically as political. They haven't quite figured Christ out and they make mistakes. But in Acts these same men repeat Jesus' message with clarity and power. They know the mind-set of their Commander and are careful to act in a way that will please him, including steering clear of sin.

Here's another contrast. In the Gospels, the disciples are basically still followers, unsure, apprehensive, men of sight with a shaky self-image. Start reading Acts. Suddenly they've become leaders who are increasingly confident, bold men of faith with a strong self-image.

In the Gospels one sees Andrew, John, James, and even Peter, exhibiting the spirit of raw recruits, hoping for the best. Acts reveals them as having the spirit of conquerors, assured and courageous, anticipating ultimate victory for the Kingdom. If in the Gospels they are immature, in Acts they are mature and perfected. The distinction is very clear.

Maybe that helps you understand more what I have in mind when I say, *Mature believers manifest the spirit of a conqueror.*

Here are these same ideas applied to the Apostle Paul. He certainly evidences in his writings what I'm talking about. Sincerely interested? No, he's totally committed. "For to me to live is Christ" (Phil 1:21). Self-centered or cause centered? You judge. "Some indeed preach Christ from envy and rivalry, . . . in every way, whether in pretense or in truth, Christ is proclaimed; and in that I rejoice" (Phil. 1:15-18).

Is Paul a novice or an experienced worker? He was, he wrote, "on frequent journeys, in danger from rivers, danger from robbers, danger from my own people, dangers from the Gentiles, danger in the city, danger in the wilderness, danger at sea, danger from false brethren; in toil and hardship, through many a sleepless night, in hunger and thirst, often without food, in cold and exposure" (2 Cor. 11:26-27).

Was Paul still somewhat confused about his message? "For I am not ashamed of the gospel: it is the power of God for salvation, to every one who has faith" (Rom. 1:16). Was he a vacillating follower or a leader with a strong self-image? "Brethren, join in imitating me, and mark those who so live as you have an example in us" (Phil. 3:17).

Did Paul manifest the spirit of a conqueror? "Who shall separate us from the love of Christ? Shall tribulation, or distress, or persecution, or famine, or nakedness, or peril, or sword? . . . No! In all these things we are more than conquerors through him who loved us" (Rom. 8:35-37).

Once again I repeat with Scripture as my base, *Mature believers manifest the spirit of a conqueror.*

Because we are working with a military term, we might say the difference is the same as that between a sincere but young three-year enlistee and a tough, long-term career man. The glory seeker versus the true patriot; the novice, never really having faced a battle, compared to an experienced infantryman, seasoned by combat. The flavor of the term *spirit of a conqueror* is one of a soldier who knows his strength, understands his weapon, and has a healthy respect for the power of the enemy. But because the drumbeat of the cause rumbles deep within him, his mind is set, regardless of the cost. There's work to be done, a prize to be won. Therefore, let us press on!

Does that give you a feel of what I have in mind? My contention is that there are very few such people to be found anymore in the ranks of the church. Because of this, the cause of Christ is hurting badly.

Most Christians of today's generation still exhibit at best the heart of an eager new recruit. Sincerely interested? Yes. But immature, insecure, self-centered, confused over the nature of the war and its true objectives. Made up of followers, not leaders, the troops are fragmented.

Whatever happened to such driven men and women? People with the spirit of a conqueror were not pygmies at prayer. They weren't ignorant regarding God's Word, insensitive to the Holy Spirit's promptings, unaware that fierce warfare wages daily between spiritual powers. They didn't put personal interests above Kingdom values. Far from being timid or overly cautious, it's reported that they:

> Through faith conquered kingdoms, enforced justice, received promises, stopped the mouths of lions, quenched raging fire, escaped the edge of the sword, won strength out of weakness, became mighty in war, put foreign armies to flight. Women received their dead by resurrection. Some were tortured, refusing to accept release, that they might rise again to a better life. Others suffered mocking and scourging, and even chains and imprisonment. They were stoned, they were sawn in two, they were killed with the sword; they went about in skins of sheep and goats, destitute, afflicted, ill-treated, of whom the world was not worthy" (Heb. 11:33-38).

(Clap! Clap!) "You tell 'em David, it's true, and I like it when you get all fired up!"

Wait a minute, I wasn't "telling 'em" anything. I was talking to *you* when I said there weren't enough Christians around anymore with a spirit of a conqueror. The frustrating thing is that the problem is so gigantic I don't even know what to tell you to do about it. Personally, I don't show the spirit of a conqueror myself as much as I would like to, but there are a few areas that have fallen into line.

I wonder if you are open to some radical changes— for instance, going to bed thirty minutes or an hour sooner each night in order to rise that same amount of time earlier the next day and put in some serious study of Scripture? How about charting your tv viewing and not allowing yourself more than two or three hours a week, maximum! Why not arrive at church fifteen minutes early on Sunday so you're actually prepared to worship? Sacrifice in your giving to help support worthy ministries? Vow to do whatever it takes to assure a strong marriage and family? Find a more mature believer who can tutor you in areas where you need to grow? Zero in on a key temptation and determine to see victory over it in the next month? Develop an interest in foreign missions just because it's important? Privately resurrect some of the hymns of the past that speak of warfare to counterbalance today's great emphasis in music on personal experience? Cry out from the depths of your heart, "God, my heart is cold. I need help!"

Can the tide be turned without this spirit of a conqueror? I think not, but I fear the church no longer has volunteers sufficient to match the confrontation the enemy has to offer.

3

THE POSSIBILITY OF SOMETHING BETTER

For a good number of years I've been studying about times of revival in the church. Recently, I finished my second reading of a book about the great moving of God in America in 1857-58. Those incredible days were characterized by noonday prayer meetings in cities all around the country. What it meant in terms of new converts is a story in itself. At high tide it was estimated that conversions were running as high as 50,000 a week.

Even more interesting to me is the fact that many ministers were placing a strong emphasis on the concept of perfection. Perfection is a scriptural word. Granted, it appears more often in the King James version than it does in more modern translations, but even so, here are several familiar verses from a contemporary version where the term appears.

"You, therefore, must be *perfect*, as your heavenly Father is *perfect*" (Matt. 5:48). Let steadfastness have its full effect, that you may be *perfect* and complete, lacking in nothing" (James 1:4). "There is no fear in love, but *perfect* love casts out fear. For fear has to do with punishment, and he who fears is not *perfected* in love" (1 John 4:18).

Because people read different meanings into the word, the idea of "spiritual perfection" today often precipitates arguments. Suffice it to say that the main message preached in that earlier era of revival didn't usually propound that believers would be untouchable in regard to sin. But the pulpiteers certainly held up the possibility of a life in Christ beyond just meager fare, and I like that.

In fact, I feel strongly that such sermons need to capture the minds and hearts of God's people once again. We're almost conditioned to failure. "Yes, Jesus will come into your life and forgive you. That's nice, but don't expect too much." I've heard any number of people say that in one way or another. "I mean, I'm not that different from what I was," they continue, "and I don't really expect the future to hold any major adjustments for me either." That kind of attitude deeply distresses me.

Had you been a churchgoer in the middle of the last century, it's very likely you would have heard the theme that Christ, through his Spirit, was not only desirous but capable of bringing about a radical change in who you were and how you lived. Evil habits didn't have to have a stranglehold on you. Tattered relationships could be mended. The very love of Christ could characterize you, and you could expect to be a markedly better person as a result of following him. Together with fellow brothers and sisters, you would have envisioned your-selves as profoundly affecting the world for good.

My prayer is that somehow this optimism will again permeate God's people. Certainly the New Testament reflects such a spirit. "That you may know . . . what is the immeasurable greatness of his power in us who believe, according to the working of his great might which he accomplished in Christ when he raised him from the dead" (Eph. 1:18-20). "Therefore, if anyone is in Christ, he is a new creation; the old has passed away, behold, the new has come" (2 Cor. 5:17). If this is God's truth, why is the change hardly recognizable in so many cases?

Apparently this is a problem Paul identified when he composed the Epistle to the Romans. Portions of the letter might have been addressed "To Christians living below their potential." In fact, Paul personally writes, "For I do not do the good I want, but the evil I do not want is what I do" (Rom. 7:19). His long letter, however, is certainly not one of defeat but victory! His appeal to his readers to "present your bodies as a living sacrifice, holy and acceptable to God, which is your spiritual worship" (Rom. 12:1) is pivital. If this theme of Paul's could be understood and put into practice today, a noticeable change would very quickly be apparent throughout the ranks of Christ.

Last summer some close friends in Michigan invited our family to use their home for a vacation spot. Located in a wooded area near a lake, the setting was perfect. If we would just let them know when we could come, they would vacation somewhere else the same week and the house would be ours. We worked out a date and when we arrived their family took us on a tour of the rooms. Little Stephen showed Joel and Jeremy his toys and where he slept. Christy turned her things over to Melissa for the week and J. D. did the same for Randy. Marilyn explained details about the kitchen to Karen and Doug showed me how to operate the boat. We shared a meal together and then they were gone and the house was literally ours to do with as we pleased. We relaxed and had a great time.

Now I presume our host family could have come back unexpectedly at any moment and reneged on their offer, "Okay, okay! Who ate all my favorite cereal!" or "I've had it with you sloppy Mainses. Look! Someone's been tracking mud into the downstairs den. Now out, all of you!" Of course, this didn't occur. We were loved and trusted, and the house was ours to do with as we pleased.

In a sense, this is what Paul is saying in Romans 12:1. Instead of a house, however, he's asking that you turn over your body. As the Amplified Bible puts it, he begs you, "in view of [all] the mercies of God, to make a decisive dedication of your bodies—presenting all your members and faculties—as a living sacrifice."

In other words, Paul is saying, I want you to consciously let Christ know that this day your body is being made available for him to live in and use as he chooses. Mentally take him on a tour through the various parts and give each area over to him. "Jesus, here's my tongue. I give it to you this day to say with it what you want. It's yours to use as you please at any time in the hours ahead. Here are my hands. They're yours also, to bless others or to comfort or to perform acts of kindness as you direct. My mind belongs to you as part of my offer too." And so on.

What do you think Christ would do if your body were his to live in as he pleased? Would he get rid of some of the junk around the house that shouldn't be there? Then let him! Offered control of your being, would he act differently toward your spouse? Maybe he would fast and pray. As I allow him to use who I am for his desires, I grow immensely in my faith. And taking things a day at a time I have a pretty good idea of what he wants from me.

Conversely, sensing he holds wishes contrary to my desires, I might return and renege on my offer, saying "Hold on now, just a minute! That's not what I had in mind when I invited you to take over, Christ. I would never use my body to be a servant to such a person. You're welcome to it for a lot of purposes, but that's definitely not one of them!" Or, "I've always enjoyed this habit, but our exchange is making me feel very inhibited about it. Sorry this area is off limits for you, Jesus." As time goes on, so many restrictions are added to the invitation, he's hardly being treated as a loved and trusted guest any more, and his influence is restrained because he's not one to impose.

This restraint is one reason that many who have invited Christ to indwell their lives now have so little joy in the relationship. If you're in that category and wonder what went wrong, let me suggest a quick remedy. Right now, offer your body to Christ to use this day as he pleases, and as you by faith sense what he would do if given control of your faculties, respond to him in obedience. I guarantee the spiritual juices will begin flowing once again.

That believer who attempts to honor every request Christ makes of his or her personage will know spiritual growth by leaps and bounds. "Jesus, live today in me as you please. Accomplish priorities you have in mind. My being is given over to you." I'm convinced such a prayer will result in a whole new level of living for anyone sincerely meaning it.

In Paul's words from Romans 12:1-2:

> I appeal to you therefore, brethren, by the mercies of God, to present your bodies as a living sacrifice, holy and acceptable to God, which is your spiritual worship. Do not be conformed to this world, but be transformed by the renewal of your mind, that you may prove what is the will of God, what is good and acceptable [now here's that word again] and *perfect*.

In a sentence, *New Testament perfection* (or living in a way that's acceptable and good to God) *is attained as Christians make their bodies available to God.*

Do you wish to experience a new spiritual breeze blowing across your life? If so, when you've finished reading, tell the Lord in quietness that by your invitation he has control of every part of your body today to use in whatever way he wants, and that it's your purpose to fulfill his desires as they become clear to you. You won't renege. This is where personal perfection (though not sinlessness) begins.

Do you long with me for revival in our times? For a mighty demonstration of God at work among his people? For another period of the church triumphant instead of this continued mediocrity? Will you then be a part of the beginning process? This day, will you allow God the privilege of using you exactly as he desires? That's when the new day is issued in, when this New Testament perfection is attained—as Christians make their bodies available for God's desires.

4

BE CAREFUL, LITTLE EYES, WHAT YOU SEE

When it comes to retaining what has been experienced, sight is the most powerful of our five senses. Touch, taste, and smell are not even in the running, and hearing finishes a poor second. What you see influences you greatly.

My concern in this chapter stems from a conviction that people need to exercise more discretion regarding what they look at, especially as it relates to sexual matters. It's not often that I speak on the topic of sex. Probably I'm anxious not to be thought a prude. Aren't preachers expected to speak negatively regarding sex? And some people probably wonder, "What does he know about it, anyway!"

In all honesty, staying within God's guidelines, I can testify to the joy the Creator had in mind regarding the love of a man for a woman. If anything, I feel sorry for those caught in today's trap of lust. Like all other unchecked appetites, the enchantress soon becomes the cruel mistress. Whether you've just begun toying with impure thoughts or the problem now has so many coils around you that each day sees you bowing powerless before it, you have my pity more than my disdain.

Obviously sex is an appetite that can be stimulated. Natural and beautiful within a healthy marriage, it can be awakened in any of a thousand illicit ways in a society like ours that's saturated with sexual stimuli. It permeates tv, is constantly in the newspapers and magazines, bookstores, billboards, direct mail, store windows and posters. Radio suggests sex and the record industry thrives on it. In fact, I'm not sure people realize how much the times have changed.

When I was in high school there was no *Playboy* magazine behind the cashier in nearly every drugstore. I didn't have to pass a display of pulp newspapers when going to the grocery for the folks. Neighborhood theatres didn't advertise X-rated films in the local journal I delivered and the evening news carried no stories of protests by homosexuals regarding their rights.

"But you certainly wouldn't want to go back to yesterday, would you, David?" Yes, at least in this area. I think it was far healthier then than now!

Our national unchecked sexual curiosity was supposed to play itself out by finding satisfaction through all this openness. Now it looks like some of the preachers were right when they insisted that lust doesn't follow that line of reasoning. Instead, unchecked passion moves in the direction of perversions and then toward an even greater bent toward the bizarre.

My personal feeling is that from God's perspective our society is sexually sick. It's not just the rock groups that treat this gift from the Lord in animal fashion. Much of the present small talk on the media sounds like dirty old men sniggering on a street corner. Even accepted programs, magazines, and newspapers regularly start the mind down channels of which God can't possibly approve. Personalities who openly oppose his standards are blatantly paraded before us. Suggestive situations that present sin as far more attractive than what it is in reality are given constant exposure, and behavior that God has gone on record in Scripture as loathing is approved.

For example, the other week this information came across my desk. A report on programming, prepared by the National Federation for Decency, of the three major commercial televison networks for the Fall of 1978 indicates that 88 percent of all sexual intimacy depicted was outside marriage. Almost nine out of ten times when sex was intimated on tv it was between a man and a woman who weren't married to each other.

What the eye sees registers strongly on one's thinking. And if it's true that our society blatantly disregards God's desires in the area of sex, those who seek to honor him must then exercise extreme caution.

Consequently, if you find sex constantly on your mind it's likely you've fallen into the trap of being too much conditioned by the mind-set of the world. You need to eliminate some of those subtle anti-God messages being sent your way. Don't misunderstand. Sex has a place and in its proper role it is extremely satisfying. But the world doesn't revolve around it. It should not be where your mind is constantly being drawn. For it to replace God in your affections is certainly idolatry. Thus, my word is one of warning regarding what you allow yourself to receive, especially visually.

The psalmist writes, "Turn my eyes from looking at vanities; and give me life in thy ways" (Psa. 119:37). Interestingly enough, David did not write this psalm, although the advice could no doubt have saved him a great deal of pain and heartbreak. How much better if he had just turned his eyes away from looking at Bathsheba as she bathed that late spring afternoon, at a time when kings normally went forth to war. Maybe the history of his life and his nation would have been radically altered for the good.

The other day a younger friend with whom I used to work was in town.

"Do you recall the old girlie theatre we had to walk past in the city to get to the church office in downtown Chicago?" he asked.

"Of course I do," I responded.

"Remember how we used to turn our heads the other way as we went by, refusing to even look?"

"Sure."

"That was a good lesson for me," he said, "to get in the habit of saying, 'No, I won't even risk a glance.'"

It was true. Oh, maybe we appeared a little strange to the ticket seller, walking by each day with our heads twisted left, but my friend testifies to a great marriage that just keeps growing better all the time, and that's been my story, too. "Turn my eyes from looking at vanities; and give me life in thy way." Don't forget that married life in the context of God's ways includes an intimacy I believe to be better than anything the people who do all the big talking are aware of.

This eye-turning practice has proven of value in judging what I look at or don't in many areas now. Careful scrutiny has convinced me that much that is labeled harmless really needs to be avoided.

I'm not preaching against television, magazines, films, books, newspapers, advertisements, posters, etc., per se. I'm just saying that one needs to be careful about what one views. Because these media are often permeated with sexual messages contrary to what pleases God, we need to form the habit of saying no.

In fact, you may be caught in the trap of looking at things you shouldn't. Certain magazines you receive, films you attend, programs you watch, or books you read, exercise a stronger influence on you than you might care to admit. How long has it been since you showed your option of saying, "No more. I stop right now."

In a sentence what I'm saying is this: *Exercise great care regarding what you see.* Don't blindly open yourself to something that will do you harm. Turn it off. Turn the page. Turn your head. Turn down the renewal notice. Turn a corner in your mind and determine you won't look at anything that you would be ashamed to show God were he to ask out loud to see it.

We used to sing a little chorus as children: "Be careful, little eyes, what you see; / Be careful, little eyes, what you see; / For the Father up above is looking down in love, / So be careful, little eyes, what you see." That is not entirely inappropriate for today's Christian adult.

What I want you to do is to invite Christ to look at all the things you see. "Jesus, I'm here looking through *Time* magazine, aware that you're also seeing what I observe." Or, "As I watch this movie on tv, I'm reminding myself that you know what I'm taking in." Got the idea?

Then on Saturday night, set your alarm to ring one-half hour earlier than usual Sunday morning. Use that extra time on this Lord's Day to evaluate the use of your eyes during the previous days. The exercise could reveal a great deal to you. Are you one who should try it?

Maybe obvious grossness can be shunned easily. The spiel of a barker in the carnival peep show would pose no problem to you. You're wiser than that. You know better than to look at this generation's magazines or films classified as adult entertainment. Good. I just wanted to warn you, however, that the problem doesn't end there. In our day, the deceiver has become far more sophisticated in his approach and has infiltrated numerous unsuspected areas. I fear he enjoys the luxury of going incognito. My words are just a warning to be watchful. Exercise caution. The carny man has not stopped hawking his wares; he's just updated his approach and multiplied his barkers.

5

SEARCHING FOR A MENTOR

Once upon a time there was an understudy who asked that he be twice as gifted as his teacher! If the request seemed strange, wait till you hear what the response was. Apparently unoffended by this wish, the mentor told his student, whose name sounded much like his own, "If you are there to see me when I depart from this world, what you want will be yours indeed!"

Sound like a children's story? It's not. Let me share from the Old Testament Scriptures.

Now when the Lord was about to take Elijah up to heaven by a whirlwind, Elijah and Elisha were on their way from Gilgal. And Eijah said to Elisha, 'Tarry here, I pray you; for the Lord has sent me as far as Bethel." But Elisha said, "As the Lord lives, and as you yourself live, I will not leave you.' So they went down to Bethel. . . . And Elijah said to him, "Elisha, tarry here, I pray you; for the Lord has sent me to Jericho." But he said, "As the Lord live, and as you yourself live, I will not leave you." So they came to Jericho. . . .

Then Elijah said to him, "Tarry here, I pray you; for the Lord has sent me to the Jordan." But he said, "As the Lord lives, and as you yourself live, I will not leave you." So the two of them went on. Fifty men of the sons of the prophets also went, and stood at some distance from them, as they both were standing by the Jordan. Then Elijah took his mantel, and rolled it up, and struck the water, and the water was parted to the one side and to the other, till the two of them could go over on dry ground.

When they had crossed, Elijah said to Elisha, "Ask what I shall do for you, before I am taken from you." And Elisha said, "I pray you, let me inherit a double share of your spirit." And he said, "You have asked a hard thing; yet, if you see me as I am being taken from you, it shall be so for you; but if you do not see me, it shall not be so." And as they still went on and talked, behold, a chariot of fire and horses of fire separated the two of them. And Elijah went up by a whirlwind into heaven. And Elisha saw it and he cried, "My father, my father! The chariots of Israel and its horsemen!" And he saw him no more.

Then he took hold of his own clothes and rent them in two pieces. . . . and went back and stood on the bank of the Jordan. Then he took the mantle of Elijah that had fallen from him, and struck the water, saying, "Where is the LORD, the God of Elijah?" And when he had struck the water, the water was parted to the one side and to the other; and Elisha went over.

Now, when the sons of the prophets who were at Jericho saw him over against them, they said, "The spirit of Elijah rests on Elisha" (2 Kings 2:1-15).

It's quite an account, isn't it? And I'm especially impressed with Elisha's persistence. From Gilgal to Bethel to Jericho to the Jordan, he was intent upon sticking close to his mentor, come what may.

"David," you may ask, "that's the second time you've used that word *mentor*. What does it mean? It sounds like one of those half-horse/half-man characters of ancient mythology."

That's a centaur. A mentor is a wise adviser, teacher, guardian, and loyal friend. Certainly all these roles characterized Elijah's relationship with Elisha right to the very end.

The final stipulation, "If you see me as I am being taken from you," intrigues me. Why did this become the ultimate test? I don't know for sure, but perhaps this whole passage underscores the fact that Elisha was sticking close to his teacher near the end even as he had throughout all his previous life. For Elijah to shake him off his trail would have been like an old man trying to hide in the woods from a faithful dog after years of walking the same paths together.

Conscientious disciples stay close to their spiritual mentors. Conscientious disciples (*disciple* means a student of a teacher), stay close to their spiritual mentors or instructors, advisers, loyal, learned friends.

What that means in terms of your life is possibly more important than what at first meets the eye. If you are a conscientious disciple, I'm suggesting that you stay close to your spiritual mentor. Let me share what I have in mind by the words "stay close to." Three points:

Obviously, in order to stay close to your spiritual mentor you have to first identify that person. Granted, Christ ultimately fills that role for all of us, but right now I'm talking about strictly human relationships, such as that of Elijah and Elisha.

I wonder if you have ever taken the time to determine precisely who fills this mentor role in your life? Name the person to whom you now look as your spiritual instructor. Possibly it's the individual who first introduced you to Christ. Then again, it might be a pastor or teacher or parent or an especially mature Christian friend. The possibilities are infinite, but I do hope someone is filling that role for you.

To be serious about your faith and suddenly realize you have no one who is discipling you as a more experienced and mature brother or sister in Christ, is to come face to face with a grave deficiency. Whether the fault for such a dilemma rests with you or someone else doesn't matter. If I were in your situation I'd certainly push for a remedy.

In previous years, I remember my wife, Karen, regularly requested the Lord to put her in touch with strong women of the faith who could teach her aspects of walking with Christ beyond what she herself knew. Though these prayers were not answered instantly, in his time God certainly provided two very special, wise advisers, loyal friends, mentors. Karen's spiritual growth under them was phenomenal. Would a similar petition possibly be appropriate in your case?

Then again, maybe it's simply a matter of asking for help from someone you already know and admire. What believer wouldn't be honored, even if for some reason they couldn't say yes, by a request for teaching you more about walking with the Lord?

Ask yourself, "Where am I spiritually weak, and who do I know who is strong in this area." Could we meet a couple of Saturday mornings, perhaps for breakfast dialogues? What strengths do I want to develop? Who already has walked this road and could tutor me? Very few Elishas become great without first identifying their Elijahs.

Conscientious disciples stay close to their spiritual mentors. To stay close one must first identify a teacher from whom you wish to learn, and second, staying close involves showing them respect.

You don't ask for the attention of a mentor to show off what you're learning. Such folk, you must understand, are not to be treated as peers or equals. This doesn't mean one sees them as perfect, but they are men or women to whom you look up. Special friends they are, but not just friends. Mentors are unique people provided by God at various points in one's life, and for the benefits they provide they deserve our highest respect.

I remember a young pastor who asked me to shepherd him in the ministry for a time, but it seemed to me that whenever I made a suggestion he would do just the opposite. He had supposedly picked me as his mentor, but apparently his respect didn't correlate with his choice.

Over one's lifetime, there's a constant shifting in

who's needed to play this role, but I have one person I've never met who has long been on my mentor list. I've read his books, followed his ministry intently, and hoped someday to have time alone with him to ask my questions.

Recently, a friend reported he had been given a half-hour with this person. "I told him," he said, "of my anxiety that his gospel lacked an emphasis on social concerns." I remember thinking, "Isn't that something!" Were I given the chance, I wouldn't venture my opinion on anything. My high regard is such that I wouldn't waste the time with what *I* thought.

Maybe that sounds silly to you, but I have a conviction that most of us need to place somebody on a special spiritual pedestal, not that they're perfect, but because God has made them special in our personal lives. Because of this they deserve more than common treatment.

Finally, staying close means we must learn from our mentors. In addition to identifying and respecting them, we must also take advantage of learning from their great experience as well.

Another of my mentors is Charles Finney, the man whose ministry issued in revival in the second quarter of the 1800s.

"Ah, he's dead," you say.

That's all right. I still identify him as a minister for whom I have great respect. I collect his books. Why? Because they look nice on my shelves? No! So that I can read them and learn what God taught Finney for the benefit of others. Mentors are instructors, and double portions of their ministry can still be passed on to new generation Elishas who are serious about staying close to them. I testify to being profoundly grateful for what Mr. Finney has thus far taught me from his experience.

It would be horrible to be in a position of no longer having someone from whom you're hoping to glean spiritual stimulus. That's why my prayer has been that these simple words could help you sense a need for a spiritual mentor and think how that lack can possibly be met. I hope you will find someone you can identify, respect, and under whom you can learn, just as Elisha did with Elijah. "As the Lord lives, . . . I will not leave you."

6

THE WONDER DRUG

My older brother is a doctor. We always suspected this might be his chosen profession. He had the handwriting for it! Undoubtedly, it takes special skill to scribble a prescription that no normal patient could possibly read, yet, with special training, a pharmacist can.

Doug tells me one of the problems with medicine is that people expect instant miracles. After all, if a person's a doctor, why can't he or she just give you a pill that will take away the fever, cure the ache, relieve the migraine, restore the faulty part, even realign the broken bone painlessly and immediately? In certain cases, incredible cures have been discovered, but according to my brother it's usually not that simple.

I guess you might expect me to state that the ministry is a lot like that—lacking in miracle cures. But in this chapter I want to take you down a different road. I'd like to recommend one of the wonder drugs of the spiritual realm, kind of a preacher's penicillin, if you please, good for people just slightly out of sorts with God and effective in large doses even with the godless. At least throughout the Bible the ungodly are regularly depicted as deficient in regard to this life-supporting ingredient.

For example, one of the passages that presents humanity at its worst is Romans 1. You'll recall some of the descriptions of people:

> . . . filled with all manner of wickedness, evil, covetousness, malice. Full of envy, murder, strife, deceit, malignity, they are gossips, slanderers, haters of God, insolent, haughty, boastful, inventors of evil, disobedient to parents, foolish, faithless, heartless, ruthless. Though they know God's decree that those who do such things deserve to die, they not only do them but approve those who practice them (vv. 29-32).

It's not a pretty picture, is it? The writer is the Apostle Paul. Here's another paragraph.

> For this reason God gave them up to dishonorable practices. Their women exchanged natural relations for unnatural, and the men likewise gave up natural relations with women and were consumed with passion for one another, men committing shameless acts with men and receiving in their own persons the due penalty for their error" (vv. 26, 27).

Two paragraphs earlier, before beginning to list such gross evils, Paul had this to say: "For the wrath of God is revealed from heaven against all ungodliness and wick-

edness. . . . For what can be known about God is plain
to them, because God has shown it to them. . . .
although they knew God they did not honor him as God
or give thanks to him" (vv. 18-21).

I hold a conviction that one of the early indications of
spiritual disease is the lack of true gratitude to God for
all he has done. Show me a people who see their gains
as basically a result of their own efforts and I'll point out
a population that's also becoming increasingly decadent.
The two go together. "Although they [and in this
context "they" is every man] knew God they did not
honor him as God or give thanks to him"! A little later,
Paul will express this same thought in question form.
"Why do people presume upon the riches of God's
kindness? (see Romans 2:4).

Whereas neglecting to give thanks to the Lord pro-
motes ungodliness, the opposite is also true. The
practice of expressing thanks to the Lord fosters
godliness. For emphasis, can I write the sentence again?
*The practice of expressing thanks to the Lord fosters
godliness.*

Please don't read that as just some clever spiritual
axiom. To work at expressing thanks to the Lord for his
goodness until it becomes habitual is as beneficial to
someone who's ailing spiritually as taking the medicine
prescribed is for a patient's physical ailment. In fact,
considering how effective, how fast-working, and how
relatively painless this treatment is, it's surprising it's not
prescribed more often!

Let me share a personal testimony. I don't know of
any ingredient in my spiritual life that has been as
beneficial to me as the practice of taking time daily to

write down those items for which I want to thank the Lord.

Looking at the recent notebook pages where these prayers are recorded, I notice I've written thanks to God for friends, for health, for provision for financial needs. I've recorded my appreciation for times of joy as a family, unexpected help in getting certain jobs done, a special phone call or letter or word of encouragement, insight into someone's problem, continuing victory in another's life. I see where I've even expressed gratitude to the Lord for reprimanding me by his Spirit. Thank you, Father, for beautiful fellow workers, recovery from illness, guidance in a difficult decision, answers to prayer, for the church where we're members, for speaking to me clearly through the Scriptures, for the freedom we know in America, for God's perfect timing, and on and on. I imagine these pages now contain thousands of items.

Apart from the fact that God deserves to hear me thank him, the practice of doing so has also resulted in an overwhelming sense of God's presence in my life.

This intimacy is that condition for which so many believers long. They want verification of God's involvement in their world. The day-by-day discipline of writing down prayers for which you are grateful will effect that miraculous state. Believe me. It's like a spiritual wonder drug!

I'm afraid you're disappointed. Certainly, I could have talked about forgiveness, which is able to restore spiritual health, or about confession, another little-used but very effective curative for many spiritual maladies. But ingratitude is practically a national disease. What better place could there be to begin?

I would be pleased if my words could be used of God to challenge some to figure out how to get alone with God and say, "Father, everything I put on this sheet of paper is something I've been given which I see as coming from you. The fact that I write it down is simply to help me organize what I want to say. For example, thank you for my job."

I'd even suggest that each time you record an item you say the word or words out loud. "My job. I thank you for it, Father."

"For times of peace, I thank you. How much longer it will last, I don't know. But, God, I thank you for this gift which I experience though I realize not all my brothers and sisters do.

"For food. Scarcely a news report or magazine comes my way but what I'm reminded of how many throughout the world have empty stomachs. Yet I've been so fortunate in this regard. You truly are good to me."

Step one of my prescription is to spend ten to fifteen minutes this day discovering why you are grateful, and expressing that to God. Then I hope you'll continue taking the medication so that full health may be restored. View this only as Day One of a continuing routine of writing down your thanks to the Lord. Then about page seven or nine, eleven, whatever, suddenly you'll begin to understand what I mean when I say the practice of expressing thanksgiving to the Lord fosters godliness. Recognized sainthood won't dramatically become yours, but there will be a definite improvement in terms of your awareness of how close God is to you.

I don't want to be a pest, but agreeing with me isn't enough. "Uh huh, that certainly was helpful. Someday I ought to try what he's suggesting." All such responses fall short. That's like saying, "You know, Doc, I bet you're right, I really think a couple of these pills you prescribed just might start me feeling better, so believe me, I'm going to file what you've written in my bureau drawer, 'cause someday this prescription could come in right handy."

If today's bottle of spiritual medicine has your name on it, guess what you should do about it?

7

GOOD SOLDIERS AND DESERTERS

At the call of presidents and premiers, men hasten to recruiting stations—careers forgotten, professions left, comforts forsaken, and homes deserted. As peril from the approaching enemy intensifies, weeping wives and sobbing sweethearts are tearfully left. Yet no one calls this folly.

This is from the writings of Leonard Ravenhill, a man I've never met but whose words I identify with greatly.

To shrink from this is cowardice; to rebel against the order smells of treachery. No mother warns her son of the stupidity of breaking off his university studies, even though he may return as a lifetime casuality—lamed, blinded, permanently crippled, or mentally unstable from enemy brainwashing. In the fight for freedom, this is all calculated and, to some degree expected in the name of patriotism.

But what risk does the spiritual life offer? Oh, let us deplore the attitude of ease today in the church of the living God. This is an hour of anarchy in the world, but also of lawlessness in the church. For everyone to do that which is "right in his own eyes" is thought to be democracy in the spiritual realm. But does democracy exist to the soldier? Can he fight when he wants, sleep when he likes, ground his plane according to fancy? Can the sailor speed to the port when plagued with homesickness? No! The emotions must be mastered; iron must enter the will as well as the soul. The vision of lonely children must be forgotten and the enemy faced, so that later the soldier may return to family and freedom (*Meat for Men*. Bethany, 1961, pp. 75-76).

Mr. Ravenhill has touched on a theme that receives far too little attention nowadays. There's not much talk of soldiering among the ranks of believers. Our discussions center more on personal salvation, fellowship, family ministry, love in the church, and doctrine. But spiritual warfare is definitely out of style.

Oh, sometimes, maybe we'll sing a hymn like "Soldiers of Christ, arise / And put your armor on." "Sound the battle cry! / See, the foe is nigh." "The Son of God goes forth to war, / A kingly crown to gain; / His blood-red banner streams afar: / Who follows in His train?" I fear, however, these words sound contrived or offensive to most.

Yet it's true that our globe is literally the focus of a great war being waged between super powers of light and darkness, good and evil, truth and falsehood, life and death, righteousness and sin, heaven and hell, God and Satan, and human beings are very much involved in the conflict. In fact, as you read the Bible, you'll quite frequently encounter such warring language, and it's not entirely symbolic.

Because of my own lack of sensitivity regarding spiritual warfare, a continual prayer of mine has been: Lord, teach me what being a warrior, a soldier, a valued member of your forces, is all about. "Must I be carried to the skies / On flowery beds of ease, / While others fight to win the prize / And sail through bloody seas?"

One common characteristic of warfare is that it involves hardships. We've all heard the saying, "War is hell." And anyone who's been in combat knows how true that is. Just one battle can radically change the attitude of an infantryman.

I'm told that in the initial days of the Civil War, the new recruits enjoyed the parading, the attention of the women folk, the feel of the uniforms, and the sound of the drum. But the Battle of Bull Run changed all that. Even the curiosity seekers, who had driven down in buggies to watch the fun, fled in panic, clogging the roads.

True spiritual warfare is no different. Unfortunately, too many believers are naive in this regard.

The last letter we have from the Apostle Paul is to young Timothy, an understudy. In it he writes, "Endure hardship with us like a good soldier of Christ Jesus" (2 Tim. 2:3, NIV).

This last week I had two very different experiences, one delightful, the other discouraging. The first was a renewed contact with a former Timothy of mine. Some years back this young man had taken on a church assignment at my request, and over a period of a year had given himself to a hard work. Unfortunately, the story proved to have an abortive ending and the pain of broken dreams and failure was great. The enemy was much stronger than anticipated.

As time went on, I lost track of this younger brother in the faith, but then last week I saw him once again in the company of some of his friends. They were new believers whom he was discipling. "Actually, I think he's the real spiritual leader in our congregation," said one, pointing proudly to my former co-worker.

What a thrill this was to me—to know that this dear fellow had overcome the hurt of those former days and was still in there battling for the Lord in another city six hundred miles away.

Then, maybe to balance the scales, a few days later I heard about a similar colleague who has set his once-held faith aside. "It can't be," I thought, and remembered all his skills and what they meant to the cause. "No, you must be wrong; not the Sam I know. Really? How did it happen?" The tale unfolded of an episode of extreme hardship and disappointment, of pain and quitting, with no recovery thus far. Whatever joy I knew from that earlier encounter was matched now by true grief. Whenever I think about my fallen friend deserting us in the ranks, the heaviness remains. I too know what it is to be wounded in a spiritual battle and to want nothing so much as to run. It's a great temptation. Looking back, I'm thankful that as I stuck it out in such confrontations, God taught me some of the most valuable lessons I've ever learned.

A verse that comes to mind from this Second Epistle

of Paul to Timothy captures both extremes of my week. "If we endure, we shall reign with him. If we deny him, he also will deny us" (2:12). Then verse three of that same chapter reads "Endure hardships with us like a good soldier of Christ Jesus" (NIV).

Good soldiers of Christ Jesus endure hardships.

Those of you who are in the thick of a battle right now, stay in there. Don't give in. God's power is greater than that of the foe. Be valiant. Our Lord himself will reward you, but not until the victory is won.

Now for others who fought well for awhile but left the battle lines, I sorrow as Paul undoubtedly agonized over Demas, former co-laborer and companion of the likes of Luke, Mark, and Aristarchus. "He's deserted me," laments Paul in his letter, "and gone to Thessalonica" (see 2 Tim. 4:10).

Perhaps your withdrawal is only temporary. Maybe no one wisely warned you of how bloody battle can become when warring against the evil one, and you were overwhelmed at how diabolical he can be.

Do a brief study of some of the major characters of Scripture in order to remind yourself what being God's special person is often like. Remember when the enemy took on Job? Yet Job's a hero because he didn't abandon the field. He fought on. Would your faith have lasted as long as Joseph's did? Read his story again in Genesis (Gen. 37-50) and see if your problems are as severe. Maybe you'd like to turn to Esther or Jeremiah, to Mary, or Stephen or James, or Paul, for that matter.

Other short sections from the Book of Timothy remind us of Paul's involvement in the war.

At my first defense no one took my part; all deserted me. May it not be charged against them! But the Lord stood by me and gave me strength to proclaim the message fully, that all the Gentiles might hear it. So I was rescued from the lion's mouth. The Lord will rescue me from every evil and save me for his heavenly Kingdom. To him be glory for ever and ever (2 Tim. 4:16-18).

Remember Jesus Christ, raised from the dead, descended from David, as preached in my gospel, the gospel for which I am suffering and wearing fetters like a criminal. But the word of God is not fettered. Therefore, I endure everything for the sake of the elect, that they also may obtain salvation in Christ Jesus with its eternal glory (2 Tim. 2:8-10).

Hey! Come on, soldier. Up and at 'em! I know what you're feeling. We've all suffered from battle fatigue. But the cause and the King are bigger than your complaints.

8

REVEALED BY FIRE

What pleasant memories do you associate with fire? A fireplace in our living room supplied by logs from several dead trees we sawed and split ourselves has been the scene of many happy hours for our family. A pot of soup simmering over a low flame. Dinner by candlelight. A college homecoming bonfire. Leaves burning in autumn. Sitting around a campfire as you end a perfect day of exploring God's great outdoors.

Let's reverse the questioning. What anxieties come to mind when you think of fire? A neighborhood home burning in the middle of the night or a forest fire raging out of control. Memories of planes dropping napalm bombs on villages in Viet Nam. The panic of a crowd trapped in a burning building. I always cringe at the thought of being burned alive at the stake as were some of our earlier brothers and sisters in Christ.

New question. When did God associate himself with

fire? The burning bush. The tongues of fire at Pentecost. The pillar of fire that rested over the camp of the Israelites in the wilderness. The brimstone that marked God's judgment of Sodom and Gomorrah. The altar fires consuming the many sacrifices. God's flame licking up the bull, the water, the stones, even the dust of the ground on Mount Carmel during the contest between Elijah and the priests of Baal.

Here's one final question to think about. In what way is fire a fitting symbol of God? When I tested that question on my children, ten-year-old Joel responded, "You don't mess around with it." And I guess that's not a bad answer.

There's a beauty and attractiveness about fire, a warmth. There's also something about it that's awesome. You can draw close to it, but not extremely close. Like God, fire can be overwhelmingly powerful. It demands respect.

In First Corinthians 3, Paul writes:

Now if anyone builds on the foundation with gold, silver, precious stones, wood, hay, stubble—each man's work will become manifest; for the Day will disclose it, because it will be revealed with fire, and the fire will test what sort of work each one has done. If the work which any man has built on the foundation survives, he will receive a reward. If any man's work is burned up, he will suffer loss, though he himself will be saved, but only as through fire (vv. 12-15).

Paul is writing about the works of various believers. Those areas of service, those ministries carried on in Christ's name, can be symbolized in different ways as gold, silver, precious stones, wood, hay, or stubble. When tested by God's divine flame, some will stand while others will be quickly consumed. That great day will reveal "what sort of work each one has done." When nothing at all remains following the test of God's divine burning, that person will suffer loss. When something survives, however, there will be a reward.

This passage has been a great challenge to me recently. Since first meditating on it a month or so ago, in my imagination several times a week, I've been regularly taking before the flame various contributions of my life toward the cause of Christ, to determine what will stand and what won't. "Father, as I review the events of this past day, I desire to know what works will be destroyed by burning, and if there be any that will endure the great heat of your examination."

This imaginative exercise, even though my fore-knowledge concerning judgment results is admittedly flawed, helps me to evaluate which efforts of my ministry will have lasting value as opposed to all that might not. On some days it seems the whole of my efforts vanish in one great flame, almost as though someone had poured gasoline over them. On other days, though the flash is just as intense, it truly appears that some precious residue remains of which the Lord has approved. That pleases me.

Often what I've thought of as small acts—a kind word, encouraging someone who's hurting, forgiving another whether or not it was requested, making a child's day happier, showing Christlike love, over-coming temptation, a quick supportive phone call, time spent in intercessory prayer—though not spectacular, still remain following the conflagration.

My larger time-consumers, however—speaking, organizing, planning, writing, administrating, working through interpersonal areas, studying, correspondence, fund-raising—sometimes survive but other times they do not.

Certain days fare better than others. Yet often when I allow God to test an exhausting afternoon, I've watched it go up in flames in the evening prayer time. Why? Too much self. Too much sheer busyness, too much human effort, too much dependence on personal skills and position and experience, too much subtle promoting of David under the guise of advancing God's kingdom.

So I have pleasant memories regarding God's fire as well as terrifying ones. But the experience has been extremely worthwhile. May I recommend this exercise which has been so personally helpful to you also? In a sentence I'm saying, *"Be reminded that God's fire will reveal the true value of each believer's works."*

It's easy in the rush of twentieth century living to forget that the day will come when all those services for the Lord accomplished by Christians motivated by money, status, self-aggrandizement, sensual desires or any form of human gratification, will be incinerated, and nothing, absolutely nothing of it, will remain.

Where does all this leave you? I'm suggesting that you begin to acquaint yourself with this special fire. Before this day ends, set aside fifteen minutes or so to review the events of your previous week. Write down every worthy deed of which you can think, starting with today and working backwards.

"I went out of my way to speak to this person who

seemed lonely. I rehearsed with the church choir. I gave money to this ministry, washed the family clothes again. Oh, yes, yesterday I read a Bible story to my grandson, then I set aside time on Saturday for prayer and really feel that I battled in terms of intercession for our church missionaries. Last Friday, I wrote a letter of encouragement."

When you've finished, picture a great fire in your imagination. Though controlled, it burns with high intensity. It's like fires we know and yet strangely different. It seems more awesome and pure.

Commit each item on your list, one by one, to the flame. "I went out of my way to speak to this person who seemed lonely." Even as you offer up the act, thoughts will race through your mind. "But I said nothing about Jesus. Did I want that stranger to see my good qualities or those of my Lord? When the incident ended, did this individual really encounter anything beyond self? What will happen when I submit this to the flame? I may be wrong, but I fear I know.

"I rehearsed with the church choir, but now before this heat I see it was just routine, no different really than if I had practiced with the community singers. Oh, if only my heart had joined my voice in its praise! If nothing else, at least I wish I had again consciously committed this skill to God as I drove to church.

"The prayer time. I'll skip to that. I trust it will survive this flame. Yes, I'm certain it will. I knew God's presence as I interceded for his servants."

Time spent before the flame will help to purify both the present and the future. Be reminded that God's fire will reveal the true value of each believer's work.

9

THE LONG SHADOW OF THE RIGHTEOUS

Can you identify with the childhood experience of walking down a sidewalk at night and being fascinated by the way your shadow changed, depending on your relationship to the street light?

The other evening I went out jogging about nine o'clock. As I passed the one and only light on our block, my shadow became consistently longer and longer in front of me until finally it faded out. For the first time in years, I felt kind of like a boy again, trying to catch up and step on it real fast. Remember?

Recently the ministry with which I am associated marked a forty-year anniversary in broadcasting. The man who's carried most of the responsibility during that time has been our founder, John D. Jess, my uncle. What do you say about somebody who's preached close to twelve thousand messages via radio? A sentence from my pastor's sermon the other Sunday caught my attention. "A righteous man's life casts a long shadow," he said. Interesting, I thought, and tucked it away in my memory, not realizing it would soon be brought out and used.

What appropriate word can I give, I wondered, regarding forty years of diligent work to deliver six excellent messages every week? How do I sum up the contents of countless letters, stating this life or that one has been significantly changed because of what God has said through Mr. Jess? Is it possible for me, as close as I've always been to the work, to grasp the way the Lord has expanded it to stretch across a continent, to now touch lives in other lands as well? It's like that long shadow of the righteous Pastor Ron was talking about, I thought.

There's an interesting picture in Acts 5, where the church under God's blessing is described this way: "And more than ever believers were added to the Lord, multitudes both of men and women, so that they even carried out the sick into the streets, and laid them on beds and pallets, that as Peter came by at least his shadow might fall on some of them" (vv. 14, 15). The reason for this unusual behavior was that the crowds felt the power from this extraordinary life might in some way touch them at their point of need. The text doesn't make clear whether this happened or not. Nevertheless, the picture casts interesting dimensions on our thoughts.

A godly life casts a long shadow. Stated more literally, a godly man or woman has a profound influence on his or her world. Who can measure the immense good of a life such as Paul's or Noah's or

Esther's or Abraham's, or for that matter a believer from any age who has consistently walked close to the Lord? Such God-honoring people accomplish far more than anyone dreams. The longer they remain on the path of the righteous, the greater their valued input.

Who are the godly? In my mind, godly people are characterized by holiness. They're not perfect, but they have learned to look at sin from God's perspective. Praying "lead us not into temptation," they do not toy with obvious danger. They're extremely careful about what they see and hear. And holiness is also underscored by the setting aside of regular times for the practice of confession.

Godly people know God well. Much of their time is spent in the Scripture and in praying. Others, too busy for Scripture and prayer, may be moral and gracious and well-liked, and they may do good, but that doesn't necessarily mean they're godly. Godliness is a quality quite apart from human attributes. To be godly is to be at home in the presence of the Creator himself, and this in turn results from much time with him.

To be godly is to manifest the very qualities of our Lord, to be loving and forgiving and patient, kind and concerned for the downtrodden, longing for all to come to the Father. In fact, over time there's little difference between the thoughts of the consecrated and those of God himself, so these people become like God not only in their living but in their thinking.

The godly revere all matters that are special to the Lord. For example, they have a great love for the church. They honor the Lord's Day. They delight in the beauty of his creation. They strongly identify with the spread of his good news. In short, the interests of godly servants are wherever and whatever are those of the Master's.

We can all point out religious leaders who fall short of godliness and it doesn't mean what they're doing isn't important. Their lack simply indicates that they don't fit into this precise category.

A godly life casts a long shadow. It's a life like Peter's—not perfect but maturing in holiness, having spent much time with the Lord. The Jewish leaders knew that the disciples had been with Jesus when they saw the boldness of Peter and John (Acts 4:13). Indeed, the apostles were beginning to manifest the very qualities of our Lord himself. They were identifying totally with what was special to God. You recall their answer to the threat of punishment if they continued to witness. "So they called them and charged them not to speak or teach at all in the name of Jesus. But Peter and John answered them, 'Whether it is right in the sight of God to listen to you rather than to God, you must judge; for we cannot but speak of what we have seen'" (Acts 4:18-20). It's no wonder such men cast shadows beneath which people in need hurried to be sheltered.

"I hear you," someone responds. "And you're probably implying that over the past forty years the ministry of Mr. Jess has projected a long shadow outward as well."

That's right.

"Fine, David, but I don't have forty years left so I just want you to know your challenge is going to have to relate mostly to more youthful folk."

Admittedly, I'm after some young Daniels or Marys or Josephs. Who can deny the value of lives that are early marked by spiritual sensitivity? God has some like this in every generation.

The other day I had my car filled with high school and junior high students from the church. In an effort to get to know some of them better, I asked each one to describe his or her personality by telling what animal they were most like. "I'm a monkey 'cause I chatter all the time," laughed one. "I'm probably a deer," whispered a sweet thing, kind and tender and shy.

One young man's answer caught my attention. "I see myself as an elephant that's gradually growing stronger and someday will be able to do a great deal for my Master." It was fascinating to hear what he said because I'm aware of how, even while still in high school, he is truly disciplining himself to know God well. Someday the Kingdom will rejoice in his exploits. Oh, for more early beginners who set themselves toward godliness!

Yet, it's never too late to resolve, "I've had it with the time wasters that consume hours and leave little to show for it. There's no reason I can't learn to pray; it's the enemy who lies and says it's dreadfully dull and unproductive. Actually, the exact opposite must be true. Has this private sin and that one been worth the price I've paid to retain them through the years? Really, now, why can't I begin to master at least certain parts of the Scripture, even if there might not be time to study and apply them all? What inhibits me from learning to love the church? Can I begin to cast a shadow that could yet fall on several before my body is finally laid to rest?"

You know the answer. What you've been thinking is valid. There's still time. You can believe it to be so. You can still identify with the long shadow of the righteous.